Learn to Read with EP

Second Edition

Welcome to Easy Peasy All-in-One Homeschool's Learn to Read course. This course will take your child from knowing the alphabet to being a proficient reader, able to read full-length novels.

The course is in three parts: sight words, practice and phonics.

CONTENTS

ACKNOWLEDGEMENTS

Thank you to Michelle Kierznowski for her cover art work.

I have borrowed the structure of the phonics section from *Phonics Pathways*, in going from two sounds to three sounds, to ending blends, to long vowel sounds, etc. I used that book with my first kids to teach them phonics. I have created this phonics section with my own examples, but I wanted to acknowledge where I came up with the structure I use.

Part 1: The McGuffey Eclectic Primer

Students begin by learning sight words. Sight reading will help your child learn to read quickly and fluently. You are reading this by sight right now. Being able to read by sight is the goal of learning to read. Phonics is the tool we use when we come across a word we don't know by sight. The students will learn to use phonics later in this course.

How to use part one:

Each day the student will learn the sight words. Show your child each word individually, covering up the others with a piece of paper or large index card. Read the word to your child and then have the child read the word to you. Then you can show a word and ask your child if he knows it. If not, that's fine. Say it to him and have him read it to you.

Do this three times a day, maybe breakfast, lunch and dinner so it's anchored in your day and not forgotten.

After the final practice, hopefully your child knows the words, even if he needs a little prompting, such as, "What letter does it start with? What sound does that make?" Now's the time to read the lesson. Have the child read the lesson to you.

You can help your child use the pictures for clues to help him read. Have your child describe what's happening in the picture before you read the story. You can also ask questions like described above, "What letter does it start with?" "What sound does that make?" You can also point out things like the "at" in mat and ask what that says. Then ask what the word starts with and what do they sound like put together. You are not, however, teaching phonics and sounding out words, just using clues like the starting sound and contained words, like "at" that they already learned.

If your child can't remember the words and just isn't getting it, I suggest putting it aside for six months, focus on letters and their phonetic sounds and then try again.

On days when there is a review reading, there are no words to practice. You might want to split those readings up during your reading times during the day since they are longer. It's also a good idea to pick a sentence from it to have your child read again, fast. This can help in practicing fluency and will develop confidence and comprehension.

While I use the *McGuffey's Eclectic Primer* for these lessons, I have edited it slightly. I've changed some of the names and some of the language to modernize it, just a little. Nag has become horse. Nat has become Dan. "For I should fall" has become "I would fall." Ann has become Anna, not to modernize it, but because my little guys always had a hard time pronouncing the difference between Ann and "and," and I couldn't hear if they were saying the correct word.

A B C D

E F G H

I J K L

M N O P

Q R S T

U V W X

Y Z

THE ALPHABET.

a b c d

e f g h

i j k l

m n o p

q r s t

u v w x

y z

Lesson 1

a

cat

rat

and

McGUFFEY'S ECLECTIC PRIMER

LESSON 1

a   ănd   căt   răt

ă   e   d   n   r   t

a rat   a cat

A cat   A rat

A cat and a rat.

A rat and a cat.

Lesson 2

at

the

ran

has

Anna

LESSON II.

The cat   the rat

The cat has a rat.

The rat ran at Anna.

Anna has a cat.

The cat ran at the rat.

Lesson 3

Dan

hat

fan

can

LESSON III.

a fan   a hat

Anna and Dan.

Anna has a fan.

Dan has a hat.

Anna can fan.

Lesson 4

man

cap

lad

sat

LESSON IV.

a cap   the lad

A man and a lad.

The man sat; the lad ran.

The man has a hat.

The lad has a cap.

LESSON V.-REVIEW.

The cat and the rat ran.

Anna ran, and Dan sat.

A rat ran at Dan.

The man has a hat.

The lad has a cap.

Anna has a hat.

Anna has a hat and a fan.

Anna can fan.

Lesson 6

dog

Spot

fat

Dan's

LESSON VI.

Dan's cap   a fat dog

Dan has a dog.

The lad has a fat dog.

The dog has Dan's cap.

Dan and Spot ran.

Spot ran at a cat.

see

sees

frog

on

log

LESSON VII.

a log   the frog

See the frog on a log.

Spot sees the frog.

Can the frog see Spot?

The frog can see the dog.

Spot ran at the frog.

Lesson 8

it   is

stand

Anna's

lamp

mat

LESSON VIII.

a mat   the stand

See the lamp! It is on a mat.

The mat is on the stand.

The lamp is Dan's, and the mat is Anna's.

Lesson 9

Tom

horse

not

he

*more words on the next page

him

his

catch

LESSON IX.

See the horse! It is Tom's horse.

Can Tom catch his horse?

He can not catch him.

The dog ran at the horse, and the horse ran.

LESSON X.-REVIEW.

Tom's horse is fat; his dog is not fat.

Dan is on Tom's horse.

Dan's dog, Spot, can not catch the rat.

See the frog on the log.

A lad sees the frog.

The lad can not catch it.

A cat is on the mat; the cat sees a rat.

Anna's fan is on the stand.

The man has a lamp.

A dog ran at the man.

Anna sat on a log.

Lesson 11

nest

this

eggs

she

*more words on the next page

in

get

box

hen

LESSON XI

the box   a nest

This is a fat hen.

The hen has a nest in the box.

She has eggs in the nest.

A cat sees the nest and can get the eggs.

Lesson 12

old

run

fox

LESSON XII.

Can this old fox catch the hen?

The fox can catch the hen
and get the eggs in the nest.

Run, Spot, and catch the fox.

Lesson 13

pond

by

feed

Emma

*more words on the next page

ducks

I

them

will

LESSON XIII.

Emma is by the pond.

I see ducks on the pond.

Emma sees the ducks, and will feed them.

She can not get the ducks.

Note: Today, we write can not as cannot.

She cannot get the ducks.

Lesson 14

holds   to

blind

Mary

hand

kind

LESSON XIV.

This old man cannot see.

He is blind.

Mary holds him by the hand.

She is kind to the old blind man.

LESSON XV.-REVIEW.

I see ducks on the pond; Tom will feed them.

Tom is blind; he holds a box in his hand.

Emma is kind to him.

This old hen has a nest.

Mary will run and get the eggs.

She sees the eggs in the box.

Will the fox get the hen?

Spot will catch the old fox.

The fox will not get the eggs in the nest.

Lesson 16

Sue

doll

dress

new

her let

LESSON XVI.

Sue has a doll.

It has a new dress.

She will let Anna hold the doll in her hands,

and Anna will fan it.

Sue is kind to Anna.

Lesson 17

there

five

bird

tree

rob   do

LESSON XVII.

A bird is in the tree. It has a nest there.

The nest has five eggs in it.

Do not rob the nest.

Will the bird let the cat get her five eggs?

Lesson 18

cage

pet

sing

lives

loves   so

LESSON XVIII.

This is her pet bird.

It lives in a new cage.

It will stand on Sue's hand and sing.

Sue loves her pet bird.

So do I.

Lesson 19

are

you

yes

fast

*more words on the next page

too
like
boys
of
play

LESSON XIX.

Do you see the boys play?

Yes, I see them; there are five of them.

Tom is not so fast.

Dan can run and catch him.

I like to play too.

LESSON XX.-REVIEW.

Sue has a doll and a pet bird. Her doll has a new dress and a cap.

Sue loves Mary, and will let her hold the doll.

The pet bird lives in a cage. Sue and Mary will stand by the cage, and the bird will sing.

There are birds in the tree by the pond. Can you see them?

Yes; there are five of them in a nest.

Tom will not rob a bird's nest. He is too kind to do so.

Lesson 21

day

what

owl

but

eyes

*more words on the next page

best

well

big

an

night

LESSON XXI.

What bird is this? It is an owl.

What big eyes it has!

Yes, but it cannot see well by day.

The owl can see best at night.

Dan Pond has a pet owl.

Lesson 22

cows

off

our

hot

*more words on the next page

they

come

grass

shade

barn

LESSON XXII.

The day is hot.

The cows are in the shade of the big tree.

They feed on the new grass.

Our cows do not run off.

At night they come to the barn.

Lesson 23

soon

sun

set

neck

*more words on the next page

way

bell

one

their

LESSON XXIII.

The sun will soon set.

The cows are on their way to the barn.

One old cow has a bell on her neck.

She sees our dog, but she will not run.

Our dog is kind to the cows.

Lesson 24

ship

men

save

rock

*more words on the next page

if

brave

boat

drown

LESSON XXIV.

The ship has run into a rock.

Five men are on the ship.

If the boat cannot get to them,

they will drown.

The boat has brave men in it.

They will save the five men.

Note: in to → into

LESSON XXV.--REVIEW.

What bird has big eyes? The owl. Can an owl see at night? Yes, an owl can see best at night.

Come, boys, and feed the cows. The sun has set, and they are at the barn.

One hot day Anna, Sue, and Emma sat on the grass in the shade of a big tree. They like to rock their dolls and sing to them. Sue has a bell on the neck of her pet cat.

The brave men in our boat are on their way to the ship. They will save the men in the ship, if they can. They will not let them drown.

Lesson 26

fall

ice

cry

did

*more words on the next page

had

with

skates

stone

LESSON XXVI.

The boys are on the ice with their skates.

There is a stone on the ice.

One boy did not see it and has had a fall.

But he is a brave boy, and will not cry.

Lesson 27

look

John

all

here

*more words on the next page

mill

have

go

round

wheel

LESSON XXVII.

Look! There are John and Sue by the pond.

They like to go there and see the big, round wheel on the mill.

They have come to play on the logs and in the boat.

John and Sue will play here all day.

Lesson 28

Jane

some

girls

roll

*more words on the next page

or
floor
which
black

LESSON XXVIII.

Here are some girls with skates,

but they are not on the ice.

Their skates roll on the floor.

Which way do you like to skate –

on the ice, or on the floor?

The girl with the new black

dress is Jane Bell.

Lesson 29

for

hurt

out

how

try

*more words on the next page

cars

be   no

train

as

would

LESSON XXIX.

Look out for the train cars!

Look how fast they go!

No horse can be as fast as the train.

I will not try to catch the train cars.

I would fall and get hurt.

See the horse look at the train?

Will he run?

LESSON XXX.-REVIEW.

There is ice on the pond, so the mill wheel cannot go round.

The boys are all out on the ice with their skates.

I will let you and Tom try to skate; but do not fall, or you will be hurt.

The girls are not on the pond, but some of them have skates which roll on the floor.

Look! Here come the train cars.

John and Dan try to skate as fast as the train cars go, but they cannot, and John has had a fall.

Lesson 31

cut

ax

pile

saw

*more words on the next page

work

Ned

hard

wood

think

LESSON XXXI.

Ned and John are hard at work. John has a saw, and Ned has an ax. They will try to cut all of the wood which you see in the pile.

Do you think they can do this in one day?

Lesson 32

gone

air

hear

two

*more words on the next page

May

cool

noise

walk

LESSON XXXII.

Two girls have gone out for a walk.

It is May, and the air is cool. They hear the birds sing in the trees, and they hear the noise of the frogs in the pond.

They see men at work and boys at play.

Lesson 33

pull

cart

ride

up

*more words on the next page

hill

goats

Betsy

LESSON XXXIII.

Betsy has a cart and two goats. She likes to ride in her cart. See how the goats pull!

Betsy is so big, I think she should walk up the hill.

The goats love Betsy, for she feeds them, and is kind to them.

Lesson 34

put

yet

call

ring

*more words on the next page

roof

we

fire

blaze

house

LESSON XXXIV.

This house is on fire. Look! The roof is in a blaze.

Run, boys, and ring the bell. Call some men to put out the fire.

We may yet save the house, if we work hard.

LESSON XXXV.-REVIEW.

Betsy, do you hear a noise?

Yes, Tom; what is it?

It is the mill by our house; logs are cut there.

How do they cut the logs, Tom, with an ax?

Not with an ax, Betsy; it is too hard work; they cut them with a saw.

Can we go and see the mill at work, Tom?

Yes, I think so. The air is cool, and we can walk in the shade. We should go soon, Betsy, or the pile of wood will be gone.

Our two goats and the cart are here, Tom; we can ride to the mill. It is not up hill, and the goats can pull us fast.

Lesson 36

keep

that

each

rule

*more words on the next page

good

tells

wants

would

Miss

LESSON XXXVI.

The girls and boys all love Miss May; she is so kind to them.

Miss May tells them there is a rule that she wants them to keep. It is, "Do to each one as you would like each one to do to you."

This is a good rule, and all boys and girls should keep it.

Lesson 37

child when

church

school

books

slates

LESSON XXXVII.

What kind of house is this? Do you think it is a schoolhouse or a church?

It looks like a church, but I think it is a schoolhouse.

I see the boys and girls with their good books and slates.

When the bell rings, each child will go into the school.

Lesson 38

Henry

kill

know

seen

me

*more words on the next page

oh

eat

quick

first

quail

LESSON XXXVIII.

"John! Come here. Be quick, and tell me what kind of bird this is."

"Do you not know, Henry?"

"Oh, no! What is it?"

"It is a quail."

"It is the first quail I have seen. Is it good to eat?"

"Yes, but I would not like to kill it."

Lesson 39

sit

near

shut

crib

dear

blue

Kate

baby

name

LESSON XXXIX.

Is not this a dear baby in the crib? Her name is Kate, and she has big, blue eyes. You cannot see her eyes, for they are shut.

Kate is a good baby, but she will cry if she is hurt or if she is not well.

Betsy likes to sit near the baby and to rock her in the crib.

LESSON XL.-REVIEW.

Henry Black and Ned Bell live near our house. They go to school, and I see them go by each day with their books and slates.

Miss May tells the girls and boys that they should be at the schoolhouse when the bell rings. So Henry walks fast, and is first at school. He is a good boy and wants to keep the rule of the school.

Ned is not the best child. I do not think he likes to go to school or to church.

I saw him try to kill a quail with a stone. The quail is too quick a bird for that, and Ned did not hurt it; but I know that a good child would not try to kill a bird.

Lesson 41

far

were

sea

tall

*more words on the next page

its

light

high

where

LESSON XLI.

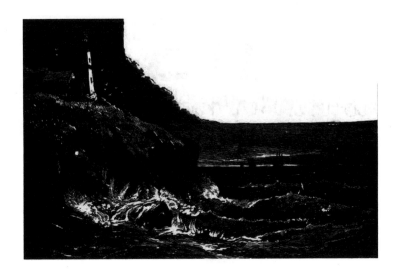

The tall house which you see on that high rock is a lighthouse. At night its light is seen far out at sea, and the men on ships can tell where to go.

If it were not for this, they would run into the rocks.

How would you like to live in a lighthouse?

Lesson 42

took

wolf

us

wrong

*more words on the next page

my

sheep

more

lambs

watch

LESSON XLII.

Let us watch the sheep as they feed on the hills. They like to eat the new grass.

Do you see my two lambs? I had two more; but an old wolf took them one night.

I love my pet lambs. It would be wrong to hurt them.

Lesson 43

head

fun

pipe

snow

*more words on the next page

laugh

mouth

made

LESSON XLIII.

The boys have made a big snow man. They have put a tall hat on his head, and an old pipe in his mouth.

Hear them laugh as they play! It is good fun for the boys. The girl would like to play and have fun too, but she has to work.

They would like to have it snow all day and all night.

Lesson 44

buzz

said

mean

once

*more words on the next page

vine

please

bee

could

sweets

LESSON XLIV.

"Buzz! buzz!" a bee said to Mary.

"What do you mean?" said Mary. "Please tell me once more."

"Buzz! buzz! buzz!" but Mary could not tell its wants.

I think it said, "Please let me get some sweets in this vine."

LESSON XLV.-REVIEW.

One day Ned and I sat on the high hill by the sea, where the tall lighthouse stands. We could look far out, and could see the ships at sea.

As we sat there, we saw a man nearby, with some sheep and lambs. The man had a pipe in his mouth. He sat with us and let the sheep eat the grass.

What fun it is to see lambs play! It made us laugh to see them.

The man said that once, when the sheep and lambs were out in the snow, an old wolf took one of the lambs and ran off with it.

I think that men should watch their sheep, so that a wolf cannot catch them.

Lesson 46

time

your

done

right

*more words on the next page

while

might

things

halves

LESSON XLVI.

Work while you work,

Play while you play,

One thing each time,

That is the way.

All that you do,

Do with your might,

Things done by halves,

Are not done right.

Lesson 47

went

got

fish

safe

*more words on the next page

fell

was

sprang

thank

arms

LESSON XLVII.

One day John went to the pond to fish. His dog, Watch, went with him.

John sat on a log for a time but did not catch a fish. As he got up to go, he fell off the log.

Watch sprang in to save him. John put his arms round the dog's neck and was soon safe on the log once more.

"Thank you, my brave old dog," said John to Watch.

Lesson 48

then

asks

town

been

*more words on the next page

show

warm

James

drives

LESSON XLVIII.

James has been to the mill. The day is warm, and he lets his horse stand in the shade.

A girl asks him to show her the way to the town. He tells her the way and then drives on.

Lesson 49

I'll

harm

fur

don't

*more words on the next page

pat

purr

she'll

deeds

LESSON XLIX.

I love my dear cat,
Her fur is so warm;
And, if I don't hurt her,
She'll do me no harm.

I'll pat my dear cat,
And then she will purr,
And show me her thanks
For my kind deeds to her.

Lesson 50

now

shall

who

queen

*more words on the next page

wreaths

crown

woods

LESSON L.

It is the first of May. The boys and girls have gone to the woods to have a good time. See them at their play.

The girls have wreaths in their hands. Now they will crown someone Queen of the May. Who shall it be?

It should be the best girl, and that is Kate.

Lesson 51

from
God
moon
nut

*more words on the next page

long

ago

small

world

shine

LESSON LI.

Do you see that tall tree? Long ago it sprang up from a small nut.

Do you know who made it do so?

It was God, my child. God made the world and all things in it. He made the sun to light the day, and the moon to shine at night.

God shows that he loves us by all that he has done for us. Should we not love him then?

Lesson 52

nigh

say

tears

woes

joys

*more words on the next page

smile

griefs

stars

morn

Lord

LESSON LII.

When the stars, at set of sun,
Watch you from on high;
When the light of morn has come,
Think the Lord is nigh.

All you do, and all you say,
He can see and hear;
When you work and when you play,
Think the Lord is near.

All your joys and griefs he knows,
Sees each smile and tear;
When to him you tell your woes,
Know the Lord will hear.

127

EP Learn to Read: PART 2

Continue with one lesson a day. There are no longer sight words to practice. You will read the words at the top of the lesson to your child while pointing them out. Have your child read the words to you. Then let your child read the lesson story to you.

Continue to help your child with a word by using the pictures, beginning sounds and similar words (ie. cat, mat). It's okay to give your child a word or two when he or she is stuck. They are practicing the word when they see it and hear you say it.

MCGUFFEY'S®
First

ECLECTIC READER

Revised Edition

McGuffey Edition and Colophon are Trademarks of

JOHN WILEY & SONS, INC.
NEW YORK - CHICHESTER - WEINHEIM - BRISBANE - SINGAPORE – TORONTO

Review the names and sounds of all the letters.

THE ALPHABET.

A	a	N	n
B	b	O	o
C	c	P	p
D	d	Q	q
E	e	R	r
F	f	S	s
G	g	T	t
H	h	U	u
I	i	V	v
J	j	W	w
K	k	X	x
L	l	Y	y
M	m	Z	z

McGuffey's
FIRST READER.

LESSON I.

dog   the   ran

The dog.

The dog ran.

LESSON II.

cat   mat   is   on

The cat.   The mat.

Is the cat on the mat?

The cat is on the mat.

LESSON III.

it his pen hand a has man in

The man.   A pen.

The man has a pen.

Is the pen in his hand?

It is in his hand.

LESSON IV.

big   hen   fat   rat   box   run   from   can

A fat hen.   A big rat.

The fat hen is on the box.

The rat ran from the box.

Can the hen run?

LESSON V.

Spot   Anna   hat   catch   see

See Spot!   See Anna!

See!   Spot has the hat.

Can Anna catch Spot?

LESSON VI.

shē păt tōō now
lĕt mē

sh ōō ow l

she pat too now let me

Anna can catch Spot.

See! She has the hat.

Now Anna can pat Spot.

Let me pat Spot, too.

LESSON VII.

will   a black hen   the nest

w   ck

Ned eggs left fed nest
them get will black hen

Ned has fed the hen.

She is a black hen.

She has left the nest.

See the eggs in the nest!

Will the hen let Ned get them?

LESSON VIII.

head   he   Matt   come   with   and

Let me get the black hat.

Now Ned has it on his head,

and he is a big man.

Come, Matt, see the big man with his black hat.

LESSON IX. REVIEW.

Ned is on the box. He has a pen in his hand. A big rat is in the box. Can the dog catch the rat?

Come with me, Anna, and see the man with a black hat on his head.

The fat hen has left the nest. Run, Matt, and get the eggs.

LESSON X.

Emma   some   pan   him   yes

do   you   have   I   to

Do you see Emma?

Yes; she has a pan with some eggs in it.

Let me have the pan and the eggs, will you, Emma?

Has the black hen left the nest?

I will now run to catch Spot. Will you run, too?

LESSON XI.

Oh whip Ben up still sit if stand Jip

Oh Ben! Let me get in, will you?

Yes, if you will sit still.

Stand still, Jip, and let Anna get in.

Now, Ben, hand me the whip.

Get up, Jip!

1,2.

140

LESSON XII.

Katy   nice   sweet   sing   just   hang

cage   then   song   pet   put   not

Katy has a nice pet. It can sing a sweet song.

She has just fed it.

She will now put it in the cage, and hang the cage up.

Then the cat cannot catch it.

LESSON XIII.

Tom   top   Katy's   at   back

look   good   doll   think   spot

Look at Tom and his dog. The dog has a black spot on his back. Do you think he is a good dog?

Tom has a big top, too. It is on the box with Katy's doll.

LESSON XIV.

sun   we   how   pond   stop   for   go
swim   her   us   hot   duck

The sun is up. The man has fed the black hen and the fat duck.

Now the duck will swim in the pond. The hen has run to her nest.

Let us not stop at the pond now. It is hot.

See how still it is! We will go to see Tom and his top.

LESSON XV.

John   rock   set   jump   fun   must   may

under   skip   bank   but   touch

Oh John! The sun has just set. It is not hot, now. Let us run and jump. I think it is fun to run, and skip, and jump.

See the duck on the pond! Her nest is up on the bank, under the rock. We must not touch the nest, but we may look at it.

LESSON XVI. REVIEW.

The sun has set, and the pond is still.

John, Ned, Ben, Tom, and Emma stand on the bank, and look at the duck.

The dog with a black spot on his back, is with Tom. See! Tom has his hat in his hand. He has left his big top on the box.

Katy's doll is on the rock.

Emma has put her pet in the cage. It will sing a sweet song. The duck has her nest under the rock.

It is not hot now. Let us run, and skip, and jump on the bank. Do you not think it is fun?

LESSON XIX.

Kate old no grass dear likes be

drink milk cow out gives

Oh Kate! The old cow is in the pond: see her drink! Will she not come out to get some grass?

No, John, she likes to be in the pond. See how still she stands!

The dear old cow gives us sweet milk to drink.

LESSON XX.

mama   large   as   papa   arms   ride

far   barn   both   Prince   trot   your

Papa, will you let me ride with you on Prince? I will sit still in your arms.

See, mama! We are both on Prince. How large he is!

Get up, Prince! You are not too fat to trot as far as the barn.

LESSON XXI.

of   that   toss   fall   well   Tammy

ball   wall   was   pretty   done   what

O Tammy, what a pretty ball!

Yes; can you catch it, Anna?

Toss it to me, and see. I will not let it fall.

That was well done.

Now, Tammy, toss it to the top of the wall, if you can.

LESSON XXII.

had   went   call   might   flag

near   swam   swing

Did you call us, mama? I went with Tom to the pond. I had my doll, and Tom had his flag.

The fat duck swam to the bank, and we fed her. Did you think we might fall into the pond?

We did not go too near, did we, Tom?

May we go to the swing, now, mama?

LESSON XXIII.

here   band   hear   horse   play   they

pass   where   front   fine   hope   comes

Here comes the band! Shall we call
mama and Tammy to see it?

Let us stand still, and hear the men play as they pass.

I hope they will stop here and play for us.

See the large man in front of the band, with his big hat.

What has he in his hand? How fine he looks!

Look, too, at the man on that fine horse.

If the men do not stop, let us go with

them and see where they go.

LESSON XXIV.

Olive   happy   make   cart   tent   woods

little   very   bed   Robert   gone   draw

Olive and Robert are very happy; papa and mama have gone to the woods with them. Robert has a big tent and a flag, and Olive has a little bed for her doll.

Jip is with them. Robert will make him draw Olive and her doll in the cart.

LESSON XXV.

James   Mary   made   sang   my   lay   Kate

spade   lap   dig   doll's   sand   said

"Kate, will you play with me?" said James. "We will dig in the sand with this little spade. That will be fun."

"Not now James" said Kate; "for I must make my doll's bed. Get Mary to play with you."

James went to get Mary to play with him. Then Kate made the doll's bed.

She sang a song to her doll, and the doll lay very still in her lap.

Did the doll hear Kate sing?

LESSON XXVI.

its   shade   brook   picks   all
by   help   stones   glad   soft

Kate has left her doll in its little bed, and has gone to play with Mary and James. They are all in the shade, now, by the brook.

James digs in the soft sand with his spade, and Mary picks up little stones and puts them in her lap.

James and Mary are glad to see Kate. She will help them pick up stones and dig, by the little brook.

LESSON XXVII. REVIEW

"What should we do?" said Tammy to John. "I do not like to sit still. Should we hunt for eggs in the barn?"

"No," said John; "I like to play on the grass. Will not papa let us catch Prince, and go to the big woods?"

"We can put the tent in the cart and go to some nice spot where the grass is soft and sweet."

"That will be fine," said Tammy. "I will get my doll, and give her a ride with us."

"Yes," said John, "and we will get mama to go, too. She will hang up a swing for us in the shade."

LESSON XXVIII.

peep   while   take   sleep   tuck   safe   oh
wet   feet   chick   can't   feels   wing

Peep, peep! Where have you gone, little chick? Are you lost? Can't you get back to the hen?

Oh, here you are! I will take you back. Here, hen, take this little chick under your wing.

Now, chick, tuck your little, wet feet under you, and go to sleep for a while.

Peep, peep! How safe the little chick feels now!

155

LESSON XXIX.

wind   time   there   fence   kite   high

eyes   bright   flies   why   day   shines

This is a fine day. The sun shines bright. There is a good wind, and my kite flies high. I can just see it.

The sun shines in my eyes; I will stand in the shade of this high fence.

Why, here comes my dog! He was under the cart. Did you see him there?

What a good time we had! Are you glad that we did not go to the woods with John?

LESSON XXX.

wish   float   tie   know   rope   boat   try   won't   oar

shore   give   pole   don't   push   drag   funny

"Kate, I wish we had a boat to put the dolls in. Don't you?"

"I know what we can do. We can get the little tub, and tie a rope to it, and drag it to the pond. This will float with the dolls in it, and we can get a pole to push it from the shore."

"What a funny boat, Kate! A tub for a boat, and a pole for an oar! Won't it upset?"

"We can try it, Emma, and see."

"Well you get the tub, and I will get a pole and a rope. We will put both dolls in the tub, and give them a ride."

LESSON XXXI.

bound	Rōṣe	callled	ḡŏt
drown	found	brāve	cāme

bound Rose called got drown found brave came

water Sandy jumped mouth around brought

"Here, Sandy! Here, Sandy!" Kate called to her dog. "Come, and get the dolls out of the pond."

Rose went under, but she did not drown. Olive was still on the top of the water.

Sandy came with a bound, and jumped into the pond. He swam around, and got Olive in his mouth, and brought her to the shore.

Sandy then found Rose, and brought her out, too.

Kate said, "Good, old Sandy! Brave old dog!"

What do you think of Sandy?

LESSON XXXII.

June   Lucy   air   kind   trees   singing

blue   when   pure   says   sky   picnic

What a bright June day! The air is pure. The sky is as blue as it can be.

Lucy and her mama are in the woods. They have found a nice spot, where there is some grass.

They sit in the shade of the trees, and Lucy is singing.

The trees are not large, but they make a good shade.

Lucy's kind mama says that they will have a picnic when her papa can get a tent.

LESSON XXXIII. REVIEW.

James and Robert have gone into the shade of a high wall to play ball.

Mary and Lucy have come up from the pond nearby, with brave old Sandy, to play too.

When they toss the ball up in the air, and try to catch it, Sandy runs to get it in his mouth.

Now the ball is lost. They all look for it under the trees and in the grass; but they cannot see it. Where can it be?

See! Sandy has found it. Here he comes with it. He will lay it at little Lucy's feet, or put it in her hand.

LESSON XXXIV.

boy our spoil own coil noise fourth
such join thank about hoist pay July playing

"Papa, may we have the big flag?" said James.

"What can my little boy do with such a big flag?"

"Hoist it on our tent, papa. We are playing Fourth of July."

"Is that what all this noise is about? Why not hoist your own flags?"

"Oh! They are too little."

"You might spoil my flag."

"Then we will all join to pay for it. But we will not spoil it, papa."

"Take it, then, and take the coil of rope with it."

"Oh! Thank you."

LESSON XXXVI.

care   always   line   Frank   row   been   keeps   home

Frank has a pretty boat. It is white, with a black line near the water.

He keeps it in the pond, near his home. He always takes good care of it.

Frank has been at work in the garden, and will now row awhile.

LESSON XXXVII.

much one yet hungry seen grandma corn would

"What is that?" said Lucy, as she came out on the steps. "Oh, it is a little boat! What a pretty one it is!"

"I will give it to you when it is finished," said John, kindly. "Would you like to have it?"

"Yes, very much, thank you, John. Has grandma seen it?"

"Not yet; we will take it to her by and by. What do you have in your pan, Lucy?"

"Some corn for my hens, John. They must be very hungry."

LESSON XXXVIII.

market   bread   basket   bought

meat   tea   trying   tell   which

A special note: The EA in bread does not say E. It makes the short E sound like the words head and heaven.

James has been to market with his mama.

She has bought some bread, some meat, and some tea, which are in the basket on her arm.

James is trying to tell his mama what he has seen in the market.

164

LESSON XXXIX.

reads   so   wears   please   could   hair   fast
love   easy   gray   chair   who   glasses

See my dear, old grandma in her easy chair! How gray her hair is! She wears glasses when she reads.

She is always kind, and takes such good care of me that I like to do what she tells me.

When she says, "Robert, will you get me a drink?" I run as fast as I can to get it for her. Then she says, "Thank you, my boy."

Would you not love a dear, good grandma, who is so kind? And would you not do all you could to please her?

LESSON XL.

does   wonder   mother   other

bee   honey   listen   flower

"Come here, Lucy, and listen! What is in this flower?"

"O mother! It is a bee. I wonder how it came to be shut up in the flower!"

"It went into the flower for some honey, and it may be it went to sleep. Then the flower shut it in."

"The bee likes honey as well as we do, but it does not like to be shut up in the flower."

"Should we let it out, Lucy?"

"Yes; then it can go to other flowers, and get honey."

LESSON XLI.

best   hitched   their   or   riding

live   holds   hay   driving   tight   early

Here come Frank and James White. Do you know where they live?

Frank is riding a horse, and James is driving one hitched to a cart. They are out very early in the day. How happy they are!

See how well Frank rides, and how tight James holds the lines!

The boys should be kind to their horses. It is not best to whip them. When they have done riding, they will give the horses some hay or corn.

LESSON XLII.

looking   thought   picking   heard

chirp   were   told   search   dearly

young   girl   loved   birds   children   besides

A little girl went in search of flowers for her mother. It was early in the day, and the grass was wet. Sweet little birds were singing all around her.

And what do you think she found besides flowers? A nest with young birds in it.

While she was looking at them, she heard the mother bird chirp, as if she said, "Do not touch my children, little girl, for I love them dearly."

The little girl now thought how dearly her own mother loved her. So she left the birds. Then picking some flowers, she went home and told her mother what she had seen and heard.

LESSON XLIII.

eight   ask   after   town   past   ah   ticket
right   half   two   train   ding   lightning

"Mama, will you go to town?"

"What do you ask for a ticket on your train?"

"Oh! We will give you a ticket, mama."

"About what time will you get back?"

"At half past eight."

"Ah! That is after bedtime. Is this the fast train?"

"Yes, this is the lightning train."

"Oh! That is too fast for me."

"What should we get for you in town, mama?"

"A big basket, with two good little children in it."

"All right! Time is up! Ding, ding!"

LESSON XLIV.

school   even   three   room   small   book

teacher   noon   rude   reading   poor

It is noon, and the school is out. Do you see the children at play? Some run and jump, some play ball, and three little girls play school under a tree.

What a big room for such a small school! Mary is the teacher. They all have books in their hands, and Tammy is reading. They are all good girls and would not be rude even in playing school. Kate and Mary listen to Tammy as she reads from her book.

What do you think she is reading about? I will tell you. It is about a poor little boy who was lost in the woods.

When Tammy has finished, the three girls will go home. In a little while, too, the boys will stop playing.

LESSON XLV.

apple   meow   tease   cracker   down   new   friends
asleep   wants   calls   knew   silly   upon   flew   landed

Lucy has a new pet. Do you know what kind of bird it is? Lucy calls her Polly.

Polly can say, "Poor Poll! Poor Poll! Polly wants a cracker;" and she can meow like a cat.

But Polly and the cat are not good friends. One day Polly flew down, and landed on the cat's back when she was asleep.

I think she knew the cat would not like that, and she did it to tease her.

When Lucy pets the cat, Polly flies up into the old apple tree, and will not come when she calls her. Then Lucy says, "What a silly bird!"

LESSON XLVI. REVIEW.

"Well, children, did you have a nice time in the woods?"

"Oh yes, mother, such a good time! See what sweet flowers we found, and what soft moss. The best flowers are for grandma. Won't they please her?"

"Yes; and it will please grandma to know that you thought of her."

"Spot was such a good dog, mother."

We left him under the big tree by the brook, to take care of the dolls and the basket.

"When we came back, they were all safe. No one could get them while Spot was there."

We gave him some of the crackers from the basket.

"O mother, how the birds did sing in the woods!"

"Tammy said she would like to be a bird and have a nest in a tree. But I think she would want to come home to sleep."

"If she were a bird, her nest would be her home. But what would mother do, I wonder, without her little Tammy?"

LESSON XLVII.

beach   shells   these   seat   waves   going

ever   sea   watch   evening   lazy   side

These boys and girls live near the sea. They have been to the beach. It is now evening, and they are going home.

John, who sits on the front seat, found some pretty shells. They are in the basket by his side.

Ben White is driving. He holds the lines in one hand and his whip in the other.

Robert has his hat in his hand, and is looking at the horses. He thinks they are very lazy; they do not trot fast.

The children are not far from home. In a little while the sun will set, and it will be bedtime.

Have you ever been at the seaside? Do you like to watch the big waves and to play on the wet sand?

LESSON XLVIII.

log   quiet   proud   pulled   fish   stump   river   father

One evening Frank's father said to him, "Frank, would you like to go with me to catch some fish?"

"Yes; may I go with you, father?"

"Yes, Frank, you may go with me."

"That would make me happy!"

Here they are on the bank of a river. Frank has just pulled a fine fish out of the water. How proud he feels!

See what a nice, quiet spot they have found. Frank has the stump of a big tree for his seat, and his father sits on a log nearby. They like the sport.

LESSON L.

sled　throw　winter　hurt　ice　cover　Henry　next
skate　ground　mercy　snow　sister　laughing　pair

I like winter, when snow and ice cover the ground. What fun it is to throw snowballs, and to skate on the ice!

See the boys and girls! How merry they are! Henry has his sled, and pulls his little sister. There they go!

I think Henry is kind; his sister is too small to skate.

Look! Did you see that boy fall down? But I see he is not hurt, for he is laughing.

Some other boys have just come to join in the fun. See them put on their skates.

Henry says, that he hopes his father will get a pair of skates for his sister next winter.

LESSON LI.

paw   polite   means   isn't   speak   sir   shake

Fido   tricks   teach   dinner   Ellen   bowwow

Ellen, look at Fido! He sits up in a chair, with my hat on. He looks like a little boy; but it is only Fido.

Now see him shake hands. Give me your paw, Fido. How do you do, sir? Will you have dinner with us. Fido? Speak! Fido says, "Bowwow," which means, "Thank you, I will."

Isn't Fido a good dog, Ellen? He is always so polite. When school is out, I will try to teach him some other tricks.

176

LESSON LII.

shed   pain   way   stole   saw   hid   eat   Nero   Hattie
suffer   sorry   something   caught   tried

"O Hattie! I just saw a large rat in the shed; and old Nero tried to catch it."

"Did he catch it, Frank?"

"No; Nero did not; but the old cat did."

"My cat?"

"No, it was the other one."

"Do tell me how she got it, Frank. Did she run after it?"

"No, that was not the way. Nero hid on a big box. The rat stole out, and she jumped at it and caught it."

"Poor rat! It must have been very hungry; it came out to get something to eat."

"Why, Hattie, you are not sorry she got the rat, are you?"

"No, I cannot say I am sorry she got it; but I do not like to see even a rat suffer pain."

LESSON LIII.

roll   build   grandpa   hard   foam   ships
houses   long   sail   break   wooden   blow

Mary and Lucy have come down to the beach with their grandpa. They live in a town near the sea.

Their grandpa likes to sit on the large rock and watch the big ships as they sail far away on the blue sea. Sometimes he sits there all day long.

The little girls like to dig in the sand and pick up pretty shells. They watch the waves as they roll up on the beach and break into white foam.

They sometimes make little houses of sand and build walls around them, and they dig wells with their small wooden spades.

They have been picking up shells for their little sister. She is too young to come to the beach.

I think all children like to play by the seaside when the sun is bright and the wind does not blow too hard.

LESSON LIV.

asked   wanted   four   Willie's   night   rabbits
lad   carried   cents   telling   fifty   master

One day, Willie's father saw a boy at the market with four little white rabbits in a basket.

He thought these would be nice pets for Willie; so he asked the lad how much he wanted for his rabbits.

The boy said, "Only fifty cents, sir."

Willie's father bought them, and carried them home.

Here you see the rabbits and their little master. He has a pen for them, and always shuts them in it at night to keep them safe.

He gives them bread and grass to eat. They like grass, and will take it from his hand. He has called in a little friend to see them.

Willie is telling him about their funny ways.

LESSON LV.

bush   cunning   place   show   find

broken   over   bring   again   fasten

"Come here, Rose. Look down into this bush."

"O Willie! A bird's nest! What cunning, little eggs! May we take it and show it to mother?"

"What would the old bird do, Rose, if she should come back and not find her nest?"

"Oh, we would bring it right back, Willie!"

"Yes, but we could not fasten it in its place again. If the wind blows it over, the eggs would get broken."

LESSON LVI.

strong　round　dry　bill　worked
sends　claws　God　spring

"How does the bird make the nest so strong, Willie?"

"The mother bird has her bill and her claws to work with, but she would not know how to make the nest if God did not teach her. Do you see what it is made of?"

"Yes, Willie, I see some horse-hairs and some dry grass. The old bird must have worked hard to find all the hairs, and make them into such a pretty, round nest."

"Should we take the nest, Rose?"

"Oh no, Willie! We must not take it; but we will come and look at it again, some time."

LESSON LVII.

feathers   ago   fly   worm   crumb   feeding
ugly   off   feed   brown   guess   things

"Willie, when I was feeding the birds just now, a little brown bird flew away with a crumb in its bill."

"Where did it go, Rose?"

"I don't know; away off, somewhere."

"I can guess where, Rose. Don't you know the nest we saw some days ago? What do you think is in it now?"

"O Willie, I know! Some little brown birds. Let us go and see them."

"All right; but we must not go too near. There! I just saw the old bird fly out of the bush. Stand here, Rose. Can you see?"

"Why, Willie, what ugly little things! What big mouths they have, and no feathers!"

"Keep still, Rose. Here comes the old bird with a worm in her bill. How hard she must work to feed them all!"

LESSON LIX.

whistle   pocket   willow   note   filled   dead   sick
walk   every   blew   lane   lame   taking   cane   took

One day, when Mary was taking a walk down the lane, trying to sing her doll to sleep, she met Frank, with his basket and cane.

Frank was a poor, little, lame boy. His father and mother were dead. His dear, old grandma took care of him, and tried to make him happy.

Every day, Mary's mother filled Frank's basket with bread and meat, and a little tea for his grandma.

"How do you do, Frank?" said Mary. "Don't make a noise; my doll is going to sleep. It is just a little sick to-day."

"Well, then, let us whistle it to sleep." And Frank, taking a willow whistle out of his pocket, blew a long note.

"Oh, how sweet!" cried Mary. "Do let me try."

LESSON LX.

turned   face   cried   low   almost
soon   more   cry   once   because

"Yes, Mary, I will give it to you, because you are so good to my grandma."

"Oh! Thank you very much." Mary blew and blew a long time. "I can't make it whistle," said she, almost ready to cry.

"Sometimes they will whistle, and sometimes they won't," said Frank. "Try again, Mary."

She tried once more, and the whistle made a low, sweet sound. "It whistles!" she cried.

*In her joy, she had turned the doll's face down, and its eyes shut tight, as if it had gone to sleep.

"There!" cried Frank, "I told you the way to put a doll to sleep, is to whistle to it."

"So it is," said Mary. "Dear, little thing; it must be put in its bed now."

So they went into the house. Frank's basket was soon filled, and he went home happy.

184

LESSON LXI.

stood   himself   flapping   first   twelve   flapped
walked   flap   obey   better   Chippy   food
stone   before   chickens   kept

There was once a big hen that had twelve little chickens. They were very small, and the old hen took good care of them. She found food for them in the daytime, and at night kept them under her wings.

One day, this old hen took her chickens down to a small brook. She thought the air from the water would do them good.

When they got to the brook, they walked on the bank a little while. It was very pretty on the other side of the brook, and the old hen thought she would take her children over there.

(continued on the next page...)

There was a large stone in the brook. She thought it would be easy for them to jump to that stone, and from it to the other side.

So she jumped to the stone, and told the children to come after her. For the first time, she found that they would not obey her.

She flapped her wings, and cried, "Come here, all of you! Jump up on this stone, as I did. We can then jump to the other side. Come now!"

"O mother! We can't, we can't, we can't!" said all the little chickens.

"Yes you can, if you try," said the old hen. "Just flap your wings, as I did, and you can jump over."

"I am flapping my wings," said Chippy, who stood by himself; "but I can't jump any better than I could before."

LESSON LXII.

chirped   never   indeed   slowly   really   brood
began   didn't   use   door   bite   piece

"I never saw such children," said the old hen. "You don't try at all."

"We can't jump so far, mother. Indeed we can't, we can't!" chirped the little chickens.

"Well," said the old hen, "I must give it up." So she jumped back to the bank, and walked slowly home with her brood.

"I think mother asked too much of us," said one little chicken to the others.

"Well, I tried," said Chippy.

"We didn't," said the others; "it was of no use to try."

When they got home, the old hen began to look about for something to eat. She soon found, near the back door, a piece of bread.

So she called the chickens, and they all ran up to her, each one trying to get a bite at the piece of bread.

"No, no!" said the old hen. "This bread is for Chippy. He is the only one of my children that really tried to jump to the stone."

LESSON LXIII.

last   slates   write   waste   neat   taken
clean   learn   reader   parents   second

We have come to the last lesson in this book. We have finished the First Reader.

You can now read all the lessons in it, and can write them on your slates.

Have you taken good care of your book? Children should always keep their books neat and clean.

Are you not glad to be ready for a new book?

Your parents are very kind to send you to school. If you are good, and if you try to learn, your teacher will love you, and you will please your parents.

Be kind to all, and do not waste your time in school. When you go home, you may ask your parents to get you a Second Reader.

EP Learn to Read: PART 3

You will complete these lessons one page at a time unless there are directions to continue on to the following page.

The biggest thing to remember is that now you are reading by the sounds of the letters. It will take some getting used to. For instance "me" will not sound like the word which refers to myself. It will sound like "me" in "met."

Your child can be reading for fun outside of these lessons. Early reader books are good choices for building fluency and confidence. Your child might surprise you though and pick up a children's novel and be successful in reading it!

Have your child read the short vowel sounds of the letters, NOT their names. Read "a" as in "hat," "e" as in "bed," "i" as in "hit," "o" as in "hot," "u" as in "sun." This is how you will read these vowels in the coming lessons as well.

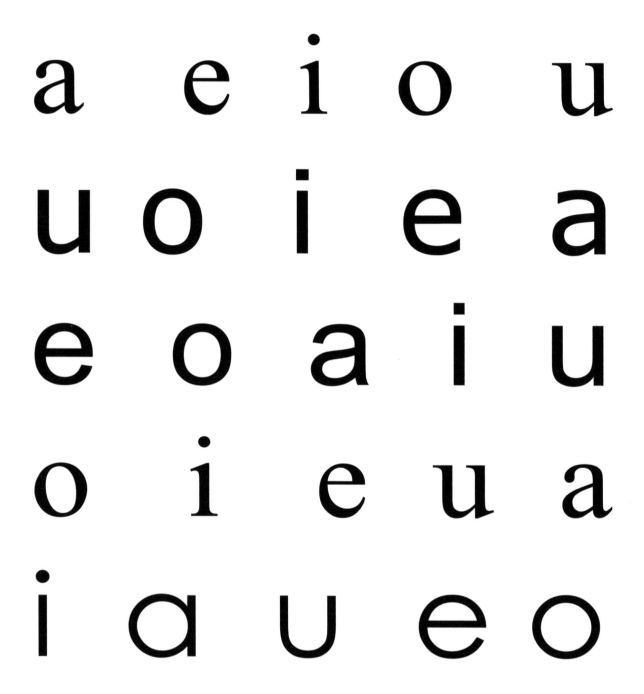

Have your child say the B sound "buh", then the short vowel sound, then the two together. Don't read "be" as in "bee"; read "be" as in "bed."

b	a	ba
b	e	be
b	i	bi
b	o	bo
b	u	bu

Dd

Remember to read the vowels with their short vowel sound. Don't read "do" as in "doo"; read "do" as in "dot."

d   a   da

d   e   de

d   i   di

d   o   do

d   u   du

ba   di   bu   de   bo

Read the consonant sound, then the short vowel sound, and then the two combined.

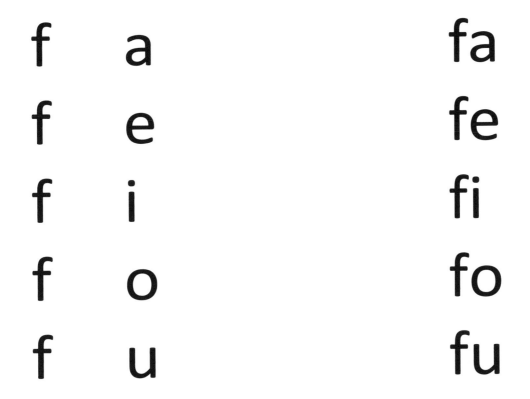

f   a   fa

f   e   fe

f   i   fi

f   o   fo

f   u   fu

ba   fi   di   bu   fe

do   de   bo   fu

da   fo   be

Read the consonant sound, then the short vowel sound, and then the two combined.

g	a	ga
g	e	ge
g	i	gi
g	o	go
g	u	gu

gu fu gi bu fe do
ba di fo du

b   u   bu   g   bug

Read the consonant sound, then the short vowel sound, and then the two combined.

h	a		ha
h	e		he
h	i		hi
h	o		ho
h	u		hu

ga hu fi bu he da bo hi
ba gu fo ha fa gi ho de

h   a   ha   d   had

h   u   hu   g   hug

Read the consonant sound, then the short vowel sound, and then the two combined.

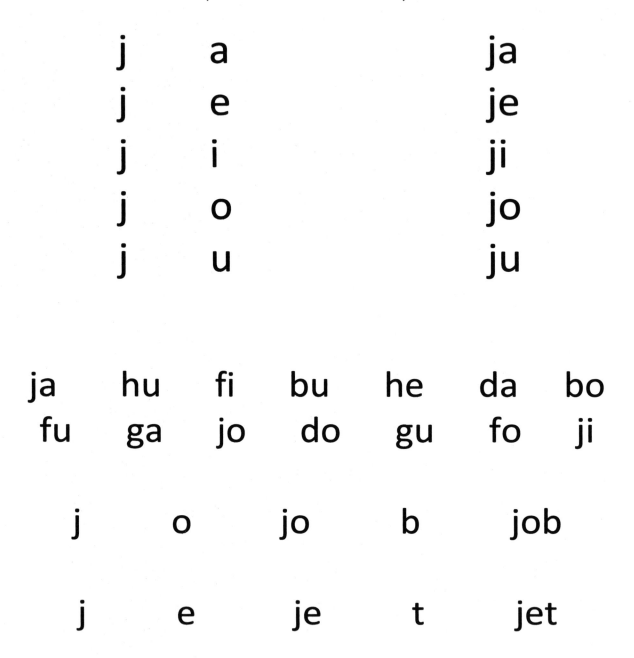

j	a	ja
j	e	je
j	i	ji
j	o	jo
j	u	ju

ja   hu   fi   bu   he   da   bo
fu   ga   jo   do   gu   fo   ji

j   o   jo   b   job

j   e   je   t   jet

Read the consonant sound, then the short vowel sound, and then the two combined.

k	a	ka
k	e	ke
k	i	ki
k	o	ko
k	u	ku

ka	ju	fi	ku	he	di	ko
gu	da	ke	jo	bu	bo	ki

k   i   ki   d   kid

Read the consonant sound, then the short vowel sound, and then the two combined.

l	a	la
l	e	le
l	i	li
l	o	lo
l	u	lu

li   ju   fe   la   ha   di   lu
du   ba   le   jo   ku   go   lo

l   o   lo   g   log

l   e   le   g   leg

l   i   li   d   lid

Read the consonant sound, then the short vowel sound, and then the two combined.

m	a	ma
m	e	me
m	i	mi
m	o	mo
m	u	mu

di   mu   fe   le   ma   bi   la
gu   fa   mi   jo   me   bo   mo

m   a   ma   d   mad

m   o   mo   p   mop

Read the consonant sound, then the short vowel sound, and then the two combined.

n	a	na
n	e	ne
n	i	ni
n	o	no
n	u	nu

ni   hu   de   nu   ma   bi   ha

gu   na   mi   jo   ne   lo   no

n   o   no   d   nod

n   e   ne   t   net

Read the consonant sound, then the short vowel sound, and then the two combined.

p	a	pa
p	e	pe
p	i	pi
p	o	po
p	u	pu

na lu pe nu ba pi he
fu pa mi po du lo pu

p   a   pa   n   pan

p   o   po   t   pot

Read the consonant sound, then the short vowel sound, and then the two combined.

r	a	ra
r	e	re
r	i	ri
r	o	ro
r	u	ru

da	ru	ge	nu	ra	ji	re
ku	pa	ri	ho	bu	ro	fu

r	a	ra	g	rag

r	i	ri	p	rip

Read the consonant sound, then the short vowel sound, and then the two combined.

s	a	sa
s	e	se
s	i	si
s	o	so
s	u	su

sa	ra	se	mu	na	jo	fe
lu	ja	si	hu	su	so	ki

s	a	sa	d	sad

s	i	si	t	sit

Read the consonant sound, then the short vowel sound, and then the two combined.

t	a	ta
t	e	te
t	i	ti
t	o	to
t	u	tu

ha	ta	le	tu	ma	bo	je
su	na	ti	hu	gu	to	ki

t	i	ti	p	tip

t	a	ta	g	tag

Read the consonant sound, then the short vowel sound, and then the two combined.

v	a	va
v	e	ve
v	i	vi
v	o	vo
v	u	vu

va	sa	ve	tu	da	vo	gi
ho	fa	vi	du	vu	ro	li

v   a   va   n   van

v   e   ve   t   vet

Read the consonant sound, then the short vowel sound, and then the two combined.

w	a	wa
w	e	we
w	i	wi
w	o	wo
w	u	wu

vi	wa	be	si	fa	do	wi
wu	ga	hi	we	vu	wo	lo

w	i	wi	n	win

w	e	we	t	wet

Read the consonant sound, then the short vowel sound, and then the two combined.

y	a	ya
y	e	ye
y	i	yi
y	o	yo
y	u	yu

yi	ga	de	ni	ra	yu	ti
mu	ya	li	ye	vu	yo	ki

y	a	ya	p	yap

Read the consonant sound, then the short vowel sound, and then the two combined.

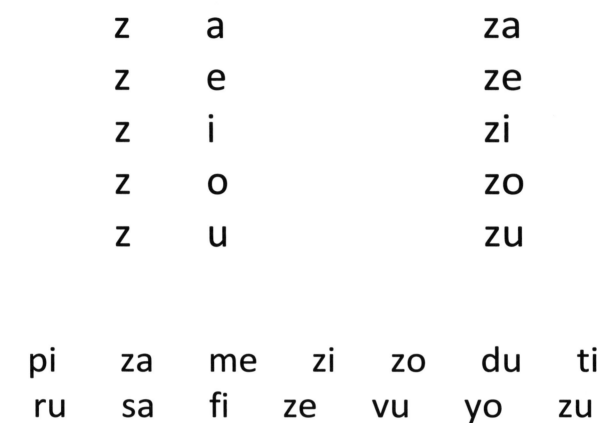

z a   za

z e   ze

z i   zi

z o   zo

z u   zu

pi za me zi zo du ti

ru sa fi ze vu yo zu

z i zi p zip

Read across the lines. Start with the two individual sounds, then two sounds combined, and then those same two letters together with different ending sounds added on.

b a   ba   bad   bag   bam   bat

b e   be   bed   beg   Ben   bell
bet

b i   bi   bid   big   bin   bit   biz

b o   bo   bob   bog   bop

b u   bu   bud   bug   bun   bum
bus   but   buzz

---

d a   da   dab   dad   dam

d e   de   den

d i   di   did   dig   dim   dip

d o   do   dog   dop   dot

d u   du   dub   dud   dug

Read across the lines. Start with the two individual sounds, then two sounds combined, and then those same two letters together with different ending sounds added on.

f a   fa   fab   fad   fan   fat

f e   fe   fed   fell

f i   fi   fib   fig   fill   fin
          fit   fizz

f o   fo   fog

f u   fu   fun   fuzz

---

g a   ga   gab   gag   gal   gap

g e   ge   get

g i   gi   gill

g o   go   gob   God   got

g u   gu   gun   gut

Read across the lines. Start with the two individual sounds, then two sounds combined, and then those same two letters together with different ending sounds added on.

h a   ha   had   ham   hat

h e   he   hen   hem

h i   hi   hid   hill   him   hit

h o   ho   hog   hop   hot

h u   hu   hug   hut

---

l a   la   lab   lad   lag   lap

l e   le   led   leg   let   less

l i   li   lid   lip   lit

l o   lo   log   lop   lot

l u   lu   lug

Read across the lines. Start with the two individual sounds, then two sounds combined, and then those same two letters together with different ending sounds added on.

m a   ma   mad man map
mat

me me   men met

mi mi   mid mill miss

mo mo   mob mom   mop

m u mu   mud mug mutt

---

n a   na   nab nag   nap

n e ne   Ned net

n i ni   nip

n o no   nod not

n u nu   nut

Read across the lines. Start with the two individual sounds, then two sounds combined, and then those same two letters together with different ending sounds added on.

p a   pa   pad   pan   pal   pat

p e   pe   peg   pen   pep   pet

p i   pi   pig   pill   pin   pit

p o   po   pod   pop   pot

p u   pu   pub   pun   pup

---

r a   ra   rad   rag   ran   rat

r e   re   red

r i   ri   rib   rid   rim   rip

r o   ro   rob   rod   rot

r u   ru   rub   rug   run   rut

Read across the lines. Start with the two individual sounds, then two sounds combined, and then those same two letters together with different ending sounds added on.

s a   sa   sad   sag   sap   sat

s e   se   sell   set

s i   si   sin   sip   sit

s o   so   sob   sop

s u   su   sub   sun   sum   sup

---

t a   ta   tab   tag   tan   tap

t e   te   Ted   tell   ten

t i   ti   tin   tip

t o   to   tot

t u   tu   tub   tug

Vv

van   vet

Ww

wag   wet   win

Yy

yap   yet

Zz

zig   zag   zap

Rhyming Words

First figure out the underlined sound. Then add on the different first sounds to make words. Each row starts with the letter B. It's okay to point out the Bs to make sure they aren't confusing them with Ds.

b<u>et</u> get met jet pet set

b<u>id</u> did hid lid kid rid

b<u>in</u> fin pin sin tin

b<u>it</u> fit hit pit sit wit

b<u>op</u> cop hop lop top mop

b<u>ot</u> got hot lot pot not

b<u>un</u> fun gun pun run sun

b<u>ut</u> cut gut hut nut rut

Word Pairs

Start on the left and sound out the words. The second pair of words rhyme with the first set. When words end with the same letters, they usually rhyme.

bad lid   had kid

mad Dan   sad man

ban sin   can pin

fan men   ran ten

bat top   cat mop

fat pet   hat wet

hot mat   got rat

ten men   hot sun   pet cat

rat bit   get pot   did hop

After this point the font will change to distinguish capital "I" from lowercase "l."

Sentences

Practice with these word pairs and then build sentences. The words repeat, so don't worry about the sentences getting longer.

hid nut   hot lid   men run   got mop

I met a dog.
I met a fun dog.
I met a fun, fat dog.
I met a fun, fat, wet dog.
I met Sam, a fun, fat, wet dog.

I fed a cat.
I fed a hot cat.
I fed a hot, mad cat.
I fed a hot, mad cat a bit.

I can sit.
I can sit and hop.
I can sit, hop and run.
I can sit, hop, run and jog.

Hard C/K Sound

The letter C makes the S sound when it is followed by an E or an I, so here the K is substituted in for those vowels to practice the CK sound. If your child has a hard time making the sound, practice with their mouth wide open or with their finger on their tongue to keep them from making a T sound instead.

c a ca cap cat can
k e ke Ken keg
k i ki kid kit kiss
c o co cod cop cot
c u cu cup cut

cut cap   can cut   kiss Ken
cop cup   cat cot   cod kit

CK End Sound

CK together just make one "K" sound. Read across the rows. If that's proving too hard, you can use the rhymes and read down the columns in the first section.

pack   deck   sick   sock   buck

rack   peck   tick   rock   duck

sack   neck   pick   tock   muck

back   deck   lick   lock   luck

kiss cat

pick lock

cup sack

cut sock

rock kit

neck cut

back pack   hot deck   fed duck

tick tock   pack hat   hot rock

ND

and	sand
band	hand
land	sand and land

end	bend
fend	mend
tend	tend and mend

pond	pond end
fun fund	fund and fend

I am at a big pond.

ST

fast

last

mast

past

best

nest

pest

rest

fist

list

just

must

FT

raft	left	soft
gift	lift	loft
sift	tuft	

MP

camp	damp
lamp	ramp
limp	romp
bump	jump
pump	rump

gift lamp   lift ramp   left camp

bump tuft   jump fast   best raft

Jump in the pond.

NT

Look for repeating letter patterns and practice them. Read down these lists to make it easier or across for a challenge.

w<u>ent</u>	tent	<u>r</u>unt
bent	m<u>int</u>	hunt
rent	tint	punt
sent	lint	pant

LT

belt	felt	melt	tilt
hilt	kilt	pelt	wilt

sent felt   melt mint   pant belt

hunt pelt   tilt tent   last sand

The duck is a runt.

I went and felt the sand.

LK

milk   silk   bulk
hulk   sulk

LD

held   meld   weld

held milk   weld bulk   meld silk

silk pant   held gift   list milk

I just held the soft silk.

The list had milk.

LF

elf   self

golf   gulf

LP

help   kelp

gulp   pulp

PT

kept   wept   rapt

kept golf   kelp gulf

self help   pump pulp

The elf wept in the tent.

SK

bask   mask   task

desk   risk   disk

tusk

SP

gasp   lisp

wisp   rasp

gasp risk   bent desk   milk task

belt held   felt mist   jump raft

bend gift   best melt   lift hand

I ran fast to hand the disk to the man.

Rhyming Words

If it's too easy reading across the rows, try down the columns for a challenge.

bent   tent   sent   dent   rent

fast   past   last   mast   vast

rest   pest   test   nest   best

bust   dust   rust   must   just

gift   lift   rift   sift

damp   lamp   camp   ramp

Y

These words add -y without changing.

sand	sandy
milk	milky
pest	pesty
jump	jumpy

These words change their spelling. How?

fun	funny
sun	sunny
run	runny
mud	muddy
pup	puppy
dad	daddy

Y

silly Bobby

funny Penny

sandy Sammy

fuzzy Andy

muddy buddy

rusty daddy

milky nanny

lumpy kitty

sunny mommy

windy doggy

dusty puppy

The silly puppy can jump and run.

Doubles

Did you notice that we double the end letter to add a –y to the words with only three letters? Here are some other words with double letters.

bell   fell   sell   tell   well

bill   dill   gill   hill   pill   will

dull   hull   mull

buzz   fuzz   fizz   jazz

buff   cuff   huff   muff   puff

bass   mass   pass   mess   miss   kiss

messy mess   fuzzy fuzz   fizzy fizz

The one below is a little different. The "a" has a different sound. Does your child remember how to read the first word, *all*?

all   ball   call   fall   hall   tall

SH

Here are two letters you see together a lot. Do you know what sound they make together? Put your finger to your mouth and let someone know they should be quiet. Sh!

bash   cash
dash   gash
hash   lash
mash   rash
sash   dish
fish   wish
hush   lush
mush   rush

fishy dish   fast cash   funny wish
rush golf   mad dash   Sh! Hush!

The messy fish is wet.

TH

Here are another two letters you see together a lot. To make this sound you have to stick out your tongue!

bath
math
path
Beth
with
Seth

kitty bath   funny math   with cash

Math is fun with EP!

Dash fast on the muddy, buggy path!

CH, TCH

These two letter combos above make the same sound.

bun   bunch
pun   punch
ben   bench
pin   pinch

lunch   such   rich   much

ba   batch   pi   pitch
      match   catch
      patch   fetch
      botch   notch

Fetch his lunch.

Pitch the ball or sit on the bench.

Catch them in the ditch.

bunch bust buck buff
batch bash back bill   bath
munch wish wick will   with

ditch   dash   dock   dull   duck
lunch   lash   lock   lull   lick
pinch   posh   pack   pill   path
hunch   hash   hack   hill   hunt
ranch   rash   rack   rust   risk
match   mash   math   must

candy is yummy   happy math
windy path   sandy ditch

The sun set in the west.

This dish is rich.

Milk with lunch is best.

ING

d	ing	ding
k	ing	king
r	ing	ring
s	ing	sing
th	ing	thing

The king can sing.

ANG

b	ang	bang
g	ang	gang
h	ang	hang
r	ang	rang
s	ang	sang

The gang sang.

UNG

h	ung	hung
r	ung	rung
s	ung	sung

ONG

b	ong	bong
d	ong	dong
l	ong	long
s	ong	song

Sing a long song. I sang a long song.

Hang on a rung. I hung on a rung.

ding dong ping pong King Kong

ING

bang ing	banging
jump ing	jumping
sing ing	singing
long ing	longing

ringing	catching
risking	pitching
helping	sending
fishing	packing
itching	hanging

I am jumping and singing.

Ben is pitching. Jen is catching.

Penny is helping and packing.

Fishing in the pond is fun.

INK

l	ink	link
th	ink	think
p	ink	pink
r	ink	rink
s	ink	sink
w	ink	wink

w ink   wink   ing   winking

ANK

b	ank	bank		r	ank	rank
s	ank	sank		t	ank	tank
y	ank	yank		th	ank	thank

I am thinking.

I am thanking Jen.

The bank is pink. The rink is red.

UNK

b	unk	bunk		d	unk	dunk
f	unk	funk		g	unk	gunk
h	unk	hunk		p	unk	punk
s	unk	sunk		j	unk	junk

ing	sing	singing
ink	sink	sinking
ank	bank	banking
unk	dunk	dunking
ink	wink	winking
ank	thank	thanking
unk	junk	junking

I am jumping on the bunk bed.

When A Says Its Name

can   cane   hat   hate
tap   tape   Jan   Jane
pan   pane   mad made

sale   wave   bare   pave   rate
game   gate   name   safe   dare

Notice the spelling on these next ones:

back bake   lack lake
sack sake   rack rake

made a date   bake a cake

fake name   safe at lake

bake sale   rate the game

thanking Jane   helping rake

red cape   wave hand

When I Says Its Name

bit	bite		dim	dime
fin	fine		hid	hide
kit	kite		rid	ride
win	wine		rip	ripe

Notice the spelling on these:

fill	file		pill	pile
mill	mile		lick	like

life in a mine   ride a kite

Hide nine dimes in a pile.

I like ripe limes.

I like the fine kite I made.

Ride a mile on the lake.

When O Says Its Name

hop   hope   rob   robe
rod   rode   not   note

home   code   poke   nope   woke
hope   lone   cone   rope   pole

Notice the spelling change on this: jock   joke

mole home   note in code

I hope it is a joke.

The mole made a home in the hole.

I woke and rode home.

The pole is in the hole at Mile Lake.

The yummy cone fell at lunch.

When U Says Its Name

Say the word pairs. Can you hear the difference between them?

cub   cube   cut cute   us use

The second word in each pair says, "Yoo."

Now read these word pairs. Can you hear the difference between them and the first words?

tub tube   duck duke

The second word in each pair says, "Oo."

rude joke   use tube   cute duke

The duke will rule.

Luke is rude.

Use the tube to cure it.

He fumes if he is mad.

The cute puppy is licking the bone.

When E Says Its Name

We've been adding an "e" to the end of words to make a vowel say its name.

Here are some for E: *here* and *Eve*.

If you have played on Starfall.com, then maybe you know the song, "When two vowels go a walking, the first one does the talking." In other words, when two vowels are together, the first vowel says its name. Here are some examples with E.

bee	beef	beep	beet
Dee	deep	deer	
fee	feed	feel	feet
pee	peep	peer	
see	seed	seen	
wee	weed	week	weep

Please continue with this lesson on the next page.

Those words all had two Es, so it's easy to tell that they say E. Here are words that are spelled, EA. They are two vowels together, so the first one is going to say its name. E comes first so when you see EA, you read the E sound.

bead	beam	beat	
deal	dear		
heal	heap	heat	
lead	leap	lean	
meal	mean	meat	
team	tear	weak	wean

I like eating meat.

The red team is in the lead.

The sentences below use different words that sound the same. Which two words sound the same? Which word is which?

In the heat I feel weak each week.

Dear mom, I see a deer.

I eat a beet. I hear a beat.

When E Says Its Name

Here's another time E says its name, when it's all by itself at the end of a two-letter word. Read these examples:

be   he   me   we   she

The last one is different! It has three letters, but the *s* and *h* only make one sound.

O can do this as well—no, go, so, but not to or do!

She is eating a red beet.

I can hear mine beating.

He will reach home so fast.

He is teaching pitching.

We ride miles on neat bikes.

No, bake a cube cake and feed me it.

Go dig a hole and fill it back in with mud.

Do not be here late!

When O Says Its Name

Here's a time when O says its name when it is written all by itself. Read these examples:

old   bold   fold   gold
hold   mold   sold   told
bolt   colt   host   most

The lime is old and moldy.

Take hold of his hand.

The most fun is running and jumping.

Fold it and put it here.

It is windy and cold inside!

Hosting him, I am told, is bold.

He mines for gold here.

The colt has fun running fast.

When I Says Its Name

Read these examples where I says its name:

find   hind   kind
mind   mild   wild

Here are two similar examples with I and O:

tiny   pony

The kind, old man is Dan.

The wild, tiny boy is Dave.

His pony is mild and his fish is sick.

His mind is quick and his feet, fast.

Can she find me here in this shop?

Be kind to him.

The moldy roll will make me sick.

We told him kindly to be here at sun up.

Long and Short

Read these examples with words with both the long and short vowel sounds. When the vowel says its name, we call that the long vowel sound.

Will he tell a tall tale?

Hug a cute puppy and kick a tire.

Pop in at home and eat lunch.

His dad has a job at home.

His big kick will win the game.

Sit with me here and sip hot tea.

His cat will gulp a bug in the sun.

It is time to go, so ride home.

The lone kid sat and ate.

At the game, catch the ball in the mitt.

ING

When we added E onto the end of short words like *bit*, making it *bite*, the E made the I say its name.

To make the word bite – ing, we write *biting*. The second vowel makes the first say its name.

But sometimes we don't want the vowel to say its name!
To write hug – ing, we write *hugging*. We put in a double letter to keep the vowels apart so the second vowel doesn't make the first vowel says its name.

Read these examples of double letter words:

bed   bedding
bet   betting
fan   fanning
fit   fitting
get   getting
hop   hopping
hum   humming

Please continue with this lesson on the next page.

jig   jigging
let   letting
map   mapping
mop   mopping
pop   popping

The words below don't need an extra letter. Why?

limp   limping
jump   jumping
bump   bumping
help   helping
tell   telling

I like telling time.

I like helping with mopping.

The hopping and jumping game is fun.

I must get the puppy bedding.

ED

Now we are going to take some of these same words and add an ED to the end of them.

These words you say with a "D" sound on the end.

fan	fanning	fanned
hum	humming	hummed
jig	jigging	jigged
bag	bagging	bagged
ban	banning	banned
tan	tanning	tanned

These words you say with a "T" sound on the end.

mop	mopping	mopped
pop	popping	popped
limp	limping	limped
jump	jumping	jumped
bump	bumping	bumped
help	helping	helped
hop	hopping	hopped
map	mapping	mapped

continued…

These words you say with an "ED" sound at the end.

fit	fitting	fitted
melt	melting	melted
end	ending	ended

He helped with fitting the hat.

He fanned me to make me cold.

I bumped into the desk and the milk fell.

She melted the butter to make the cake.

ER

Now we are going to take some of these same words and add an ER to the end of them.

fan	fanning	fanned	fanner
hum	humming	hummed	hummer
bag	bagging	bagged	bagger
tan	tanning	tanned	tanner
hop	hopping	hopped	hopper
limp	limping	limped	limper
jump	jumping	jumped	jumper
help	helping	helped	helper
kick	kicking	kicked	kicker

Did you notice all the double letters? They don't all have double letters, which ones do? They *do* all have two letters between the first and second vowel.

Please continue this lesson on the next page.

The bagger bagged the meat and milk.

The tanner tanned the hide of a deer.

I am a helper at home with mom and dad.

The kicker is kicking the ball.

He hummed and ate all the cake.

The fastest hopper is the winner.

Lending a hand helps a lot.

Winter is wetter than summer.

ING and ER and ED

Sometimes we want the first vowel to say its name, like with *biting.* We want the I to say its name. If we added a double T, what would it say?

bit-ting – That's not a word!

Read these examples with NO double letters, so all of the first vowels say their name.

bite ing	biting	biter	
ride ing	riding	rider	
mine ing	mining	miner	

mope	moping	moper	moped
vote	voting	voter	voted
rope	roping	roper	roped
hate	hating	hater	hated
rate	rating	rater	rated
rake	raking	raker	raked

Please continue with this lesson on the next page.

read	reading	reader	
lead	leading	leader	
bead	beading	beader	beaded
leap	leaping	leaper	leaped

Reading is fun.

I voted. I like the leader.

Riding fast, we feel the wind go past.

The miner is at his home near the mine.

Long and Short

hop	hopping	hopped
hope	hoping	hoped

mop	mopping	mopped
mope	moping	moped

tap	tapping	tapped
tape	taping	taped

back	backing	backed
bake	baking	baked

fill	filling	filled
file	filing	filed

Read the sentences.

I am a renter and I rented a home here.

I taped the sheet up to make a tent.

The cake filling is yummy.

I am hoping I am hopping the fastest.

He backed up and fell in the ditch!

He moped all the time.

The rider must help us.

He is lending me a hand by helping to mop.

Summer is sunny and winter is chilly.

Chunk that Word!

You can break up big words and read their parts.

itself	it-self
cannot	can-not
bedtime	bed-time
sunset	sun-set
forget	for-get
salamander	sal-a-man-der
cupcake	cup-cake
baseball	base-ball
rabbit	rab-bit
pumpkin	pump-kin
talented	tal-en-ted

More than One

Add an S

ball	balls	wall	walls
bike	bikes	rake	rakes
cat	cats	hat	hats
dog	dogs	mug	mugs
hit	hits	pit	pits
kid	kids	bid	bids
lock	locks	rock	rocks

Add an ES

patch	patches	pitch	pitches
wish	wishes	rash	rashes
buzz	buzzes	fizz	fizzes
lunch	lunches	bunch	bunches

X

box (rhymes with socks)
fox
fix
fax
tax (sounds like tacks)
tux

exit   ex-it
expect   ex-pect

exterminate ex-ter-min-ate

I expect him to fix his box.

I came in the exit!

SH

shut	ship	shape	shop
share	shot	shell	shade
shake	shave	she	shed
sheet	shelf	Sherry	shellfish

shock	shocked	shocking	shocker
shift	shifted	shifting	
shine	shined	shining	

I expect to find that the shearer shaved the sheep.

The sun is shining, so I am sitting in the shade.

SH

wish shape   fish ship   shake shop

sell shell   rush shot   she gushed

Sherry shined   shudder shock

yummy dish   sunny shape

I rushed to the shop; I needed dishes.

The sun shone on the sand and shells.

I am shining my ship.

She's shaping up.

That is shocking!

I am eating a yummy dish at the Fish Shack.

CH

chips	chipper	chipping
chop	chopper	chopping
chatter	chatterer	chattering
chapped	cheep	cheap
cheat	cheer	chat
chase	check	checkers

Did she cheat at checkers?

I got chips cheap and cheered.

Check if he is chopping the cheese.

(The S in cheese sounds like a Z. You've seen that before with plural words such as fizzes and peaches.)

She is chattering to me.

CH

pitch chips   batch chopped

ditch checked   rich and cheap

Chase me!

The teacher checked the tests.

She chops trees for her job.

Run and fetch a bag of chips.

The dish is rich and yummy.

Find shade in the ditch.

Bake a batch of muffins.

Rent a cheap tent to pitch near the lake.

WH

when   wheat   white   whiz

whip   whim   which   whopper

There are some WH words that don't follow the rules we've learned. You should just know them:

why   who   whose   what

where   weather   were   was

When did he leave his job?

Which were the games she liked best?

Whose bike was at home?

What team has a white logo? (lo-go)

Where was the whiz kid who likes math?

Who told that whopper of a tale?

Why is the weather so cold?

TH

then   this   that   those

these   thin   thick   thud

them   there (rhymes with where)

this, that and the other

These bells sing songs.

This bathtub was deep.

The weather is thick with fog.

Then hand this to them.

Those fans were cheering wildly.

There is the thin path that leads home.

The thick mud was under Beth's feet.

There is an S on the end of Beth's name. There is not more than one Beth. That mark is called an apostrophe. The apostrophe S tells us that the feet belong to Beth. They are Beth's feet.

QU

quick   quit   queen   quite

quilt   quack   quiet (qu – I – et)

I think I hear a duck quacking.

It is quite quiet here.

Quick, let's bake a cake.

I like soft quilts.

I quit thinking bad things.

She is quite wonderful.

Thank Sally for the queen-sized quilt.

Review

When is he going to see the queen?

When is the best time to quit?

What is he thinking?

Where is she chasing him so quickly?

The cabin is quiet to rest in.

Rabbits do not quack.

Sherry is chomping on her lunch.

I like this cheese so much!

Let's sit in the shade; the weather is sunny.

Which lake is the best?

L Blends

a	la	bla	blab	blabber
a	la	fla	flap	flapping
a	la	pla	plan	planned
a	la	cla	clap	clapping
a	la	gla	glad	gladden
a	la	sla	slap	slapped

bleed	bleep	blubber	blame
fleet	flame	flip	flop
flute	flume	pluck	plate
plane	clear	plug	plugging

He claps his hands if he is happy.

The duck was flapping its wings.

L Blends

clean	cleaner	cleaned	cleaning
clog	clogger	clogged	clogging
clear	clearer	cleared	clearing
slip	slipper	slipped	slipping
sled	sleds	sledded	sledding
clutch	clutches	clutched	clutching
gleam	glum	sleep	sleeping
slug	slit	slab	slush

I slid in the slush after sledding.

I cleaned it and cleared the glob from the clog.

The slug gleamed in the sunny clearing.

L Blends

clean flag	flip slab	glad plan
slip slide	glum glad	plug clog
blame plane	sleep fleet	clip clop
pluck blob	blip bleep	slip shod

gleaming shine

flipping fantastic

I am sleepy. Please be quiet so I can go to sleep.
(The S in please sounds like a Z like in cheese.)

I like flip flops on the sandy beach.

I pluck the weeds near the plants.

I am glad when the sun is shining.

I cleaned there and I need to clean here.

SM, SN

a	ma	sma	smash
e	me	sme	smell
i	mi	smi	smitten
o	mo	smo	smock
u	mu	smu	Smuckers

smile   smear   smack   smashing

a	na	sna	snap
e	ne	sne	Snell
i	ni	sni	snip
o	no	sno	snob
u	nu	snu	snub

snipe   sneer   snapping

I am smitten with the smell of lunch.

I smile when I think of him.

She got a smear on her smock.

ST, SP

e	te	ste	step
i	ti	sti	still
o	to	sto	stop
u	tu	stu	stuck
a	pa	spa	spat
e	pe	spe	sped

stick	stale	speed	spare
spine	steer	spade	stiff

I stepped in mud and got stuck.

I steered the clean, speedy rocket.

He smiled and stopped near the spitting llama.
(I put in a funny word. Can you guess what it is?)

276

SC, SK

a   can   scan
i   kit   skit

Kate   skate   kill   skill
cat   scat   etch   sketch
kin   skin   cab   scab
scale   skip   scare

He can skip and sketch with skill.

He skated and fell and cut his skin. Then he got a scab.

Kate scared the cat and it scaled the wall.

S

scan	scab	scat
scale	scare	skate
skit	skin	skip
skill	skill-fully	
smile	smell	smash
smock	smear	
snob	snot	
snip	snap	snub
spare	spit	spot
sputter	spud	
stop	stun	stab
steep	still	

I can skillfully sketch in steep spots.

I still skip the scary parts.

R Blends

ra	bra	brass	Brad	bran
ra	cra	crab	cram	crack
ra	dra	drag	drat	drab
re	fre	Fred	fret	fresh
ri	gri	grip	grill	grit
ro	pro	prop	prom	prod
ru	tru	truck	trum-pet-ing	

I hear the animals trumpeting.

There is a fox trapped inside the grill.

This truck delivers bricks. (de-liv-ers)

Cracked, fresh crab is yummy.

Drag the brass bed up here.

R Blends

Clear a spot for me at the trading post.

Be cheerful, not grumpy.

Bring lots of creamy treats, please.

He has a trick up his sleeve.

I like this evening's program.

Grab a blade of green grass.

I am in the bathtub dripping wet.

Black is not the same as white.

We planned a free trip for Fred.

Grandma told me that creaking bones mean bad weather.

I had a dream that I was a crab.

Review

Glitter is fun to put on crafts.

Slithering snakes like cramped muddy spots.
(Sli-ther-ing)

I like to eat snacks between meals.

Bring trunks to pack for the trip to the tropics.
(trop-ics)

Greedy kids do not get treats.

Sniff and smell this rose.

Grab a clock and time me!

She pricked her finger and it bled.

Clean the clearing for a picnic.

AR

are   bar   car   far   par   tar

art   bark   card   farm   park   tarp

arm   cart   part   tart

dart   mart   start   smart

darn   yarn   barn   harm

dark   hark   mark   stark   spark
                              sparkles

That was sharp! Be careful.

The bug darted here and there.

Tree bark can be made into paper.

He can hear barking on a farm.

Are we going to the park?

Pull the cart along with us.

Pride can be harmful.

OR

or   for   ford   fork   fort   form

cord   cork   sort   pork   bore   horse

horn   corn   torn   born

The E is silent in horse. There is no vowel near it for the E to change its sound.

These sound the same but are AR words:

war   wart   warm

warp   ward   warn

There is going to be a storm warning.

Was he born in September? (Sep-tem-ber)

The corn has ripened; we can begin picking.

She eats pork with a fork.

A horn is a brass instrument. (in-stru-ment)

I told her that it was boring.

Sort these socks for me, please.

Ride the horse back to the barn.

OR

These sound like OR but are spelled differently:

door   **floor**   **more**   **score**
four   **your**   **roar**   **soar**

This sentence has all six different spellings for OR. Can you find them all?
Four stores got awards for selling boards indoors.

After the storm it will be warmer.

There were no scores; it was the most boring game ever.

Wipe your feet before you step on the floor.

It poured in the morning and I was dripping wet.

We walked north while we watched an eagle soar.   (Watched has a different A sound. Can you figure it out?)

ER IR UR

These sound the same but are spelled differently:

her	herd	perm	perch
bird	dirt	first	thirst
burn	hurt	purr	turn

The girl got hurt falling in the dirt.

The cat purred when she was thirsty.

A bird sat singing from its perch.

Her farm has a herd of pigs.

Be careful not to get burned.

I got a perm, so my hair is curly.

I finished my chores first.

(We haven't learned the word my yet. Did you figure out that the Y says I like why?)

More UR Sounds

These words have the same UR sound in them but are spelled in two different ways.

work   word   worm   world
earth   heard   learn   earn

The early bird gets the worm.

I think that was the worst I heard!

The whole world shares the earth.

I finished my chores first.

The girl learned her words this week.

I heard your song being sung at church.

The card got torn at the park.

See you later alligator.
After a while crocodile.

I earn money being a hard worker.

AI

You learned that ee and ea both say E. Well, the rule that "when two vowels go awalking the first one does the talking" is true for other sounds too. We are first going to look at different ways to make the A sound, at different ways to make A say its name. One way is with the letters ai together.

sail	tail	rail	wail
pail	mail	nail	jail
fail	trail	train	rain
pain	gain	main	plain
pair	hair	lair	maid
paid	raid	laid	wait
paint	faint	fair	dainty

Use the pail and paint the plain train rail red.

Deliver the mail quickly to the jail in the rain.

AY

Here's another combination that makes A say its name.

say	ray	may	pay
lay	day	hay	way
away	tray	clay	play
pray	today	holiday	gray

Today is a gray day, but I want to play.

Bring clay on a tray and we'll play.

("We'll" means we will. The apostrophe separates the WE from the Ls. You don't read the word as "well." You read WE and then add the L sound.)

I will pay the way for us on the train.

Let's go away for the holiday.

Pray for a better way.

Saying "please" is polite manners.

She is learning to lay the hay for the animals.

A word to learn with the A sound is they.

Long O Sound

Here are some ways that you can write the long O sound, how you can make O say its name.

oat   boat   coat   float   goat

doe   foe   hoe   goes   toe

tow   bow   mow   row   low

know   This has a silent letter K, which keeps it from saying now.

I like yellow roses and he likes bows and arrows.

I know his pillow has boats on it.

The goat eats the grass to mow it!

This floats so slowly.

He goes to play with no coat.

Your toes are in a row.

The doe bends low to eat the oats.

Did they see the rainbow?

Long O and A Sounds

Row, row, row your boat, gently up the stream. Merrily, merrily, merrily, merrily, life is but a dream. (We haven't used the soft G in gently before.)

We know Little Bo Peep has lost her sheep.

The wind blows softly and the stream flows slowly.

Wait and stay today to play and paint.

Rain, rain go away.

The boat sails swiftly in the sea.

The jam on his toast stained his shirt.

The soap boat floats in the bathtub.

Mowing the grass is my chore.

Yesterday we went below deck.
(yes – ter –day)

Train tracks   chain cracks   stained stacks

Long U Sound

Two vowels make the first say its name:

true   glue   blue
fruit   suit

Here's a word that does not follow the rule!   shoe

Here are other ways to make the long U sound.

too   soon   spoon   moon
food   tooth   cartoon

Ew!   new   pew   blew
flew   stew   chew   dew

you   soup   group

Eat your fruit stew with a spoon.

Do you think it is true that the suit is blue?

These OO words have a different sound. You've seen LOOK. These rhyme with look.

book   took

IE

Here is a weird one. Sometimes IE sounds like the letter name E. There is a spelling rule that requires this. It goes like this: I before E except after C.

field   shield   thief   belief

believe   relieve   Debbie   Katie

You can also see it in some plural words. When a y comes after a vowel we just add an s, like in *day* we write *days* and for *key* we write *keys*. But if the y doesn't come after a vowel, if it comes after a consonant, we write it like this:

party   parties   daisy   daisies

baby   babies   puppy   puppies

The thief stole the daisies.

I know he took them for the parties.

The puppies are playing in the field.

I believe a nap will relieve the babies.

He hung the shield up in the lobby for the tourists to see.

IE

Now ie is going to sound the way it should. It is going to make I say its name. It does this at the end of word.

pie   lie   tie

We know Y can sound like E, but it can sound like I too. Basically, when it comes at the end of a short word it will sound like Y and at the end of a long word it will sound like E.

try   tries   fly   flies
fry   fries   pry   pries
spy   spies

He tries so hard to fly.

Try and pry this pie from the pan.

Never lie.

Eat these yummy cheesy fries.

There is a fly on my tie.

He trapped the thief by spying on him.

I sounds

Here are some more words with the I sound.

my	by	type	style
guy	buy		
rye	bye		
guide			
high	light	night	bright

My guide has weird style.

I like rye and wheat but not oat.

Go spy on that guy.

Why are you so shy?

I believe Debbie tries to type super fast.

Hang the light up high by the daisies over there so that it will be bright tonight in here.

My kids are playing hide and seek.

Long Vowel Sounds

The tiny bird tries to fly free in the air. I see its first flight.

Coal is burned in stoves for heat.

This new book has interesting stories.

I believe this daisy field is for sale.

People think that trees grow slowly.

May we please use the guidebook?

The boat will be waiting in the harbor tonight.

Type this word as quickly as you can.

Flour and sugar together make yummy muffins.

Your chore is to rake and pile the leaves.

Sue buys stew and pie for lunch.

CE

Today we are going to read C words, words that are written CE. When C is followed by E (or I or Y) it sounds like an S instead of K. Here are some words to read.

ice	rice	mice	nice
spice	twice	slice	price
space	race	face	place
prince	France	dance	
cement	cell	celebrate	celery

Is France a leader in the space race?

Use that spice twice to make the rice.

Let's dance to celebrate!

Pour the cement into place.

Paint the kids' faces like mice.

CI, CY

Here are more words where C sounds like S. Why does E come before I in received? I before E except after C is the rule.

circle   circus   cycle   cyclone

cylinder (sill – in – der)   city

More words:

receive   ceiling   receipt
                              (The P is silent.)

Do you see what's in the center circle ring at the circus?

Did you receive a receipt from the waiter?

The hot air floats to the ceiling and cools and then falls down again in a cycle.

That's a fancy dance she performed.

The lights in the city are bright.

I ride my bicycle to the park.

Congratulations! You can read!

ABOUT THE EASY PEASY ALL-IN-ONE HOMESCHOOL

The Easy Peasy All-in-One Homeschool is a free, complete online homeschool curriculum. There are 180 days of ready-to-go assignments for every level and every subject. It's created for your children to work as independently as you want them to. Preschool through high school is available as well as courses ranging from English, math, science and history to art, music, computer, thinking, physical education and health. A daily Bible lesson is offered as well.

The mission of Easy Peasy is to enable those to homeschool who otherwise thought they couldn't.

Easy Peasy has full offline reading, language arts and math courses as well.

If you want to go completely offline, check out Lee's Bible-based Genesis Curriculum.